TECH GIRLS™

Careers for

TECH GIRLS IN

SCIENCE

REBECCA T. KLEIN

ROSEN
PUBLISHING®

New York

Published in 2016 by The Rosen Publishing Group, Inc.
29 East 21st Street, New York, NY 10010

Library of Congress Cataloging-in-Publication Data

Klein, Rebecca T., author.
Careers for tech girls in science/Rebecca T. Klein.—First edition.
        pages cm.—(Tech girls)
Includes bibliographical references and index.
ISBN 978-1-4994-6103-9 (library bound)
1. Women in science—Juvenile literature. 2. Women scientists—Juvenile literature. 3. Science—Vocational guidance—Juvenile literature. [1. Vocational guidance.] I. Title.
Q130.K54 2016
502.3—dc23

                                                                                    2014042503

Manufactured in the United States of America

CONTENTS

Introduction

In the late 1980s and early 1990s, Mayim Bialik was studying lines for her starring role on the hit sitcom *Blossom* and a number of other roles in movies and television while also nurturing an interest in science. After a successful career as a child actress, Bialik left the spotlight to pursue an undergraduate degree and a Ph.D. in neuroscience. In recent years, she has returned to acting to portray neurobiologist Dr. Amy Farrah Fowler on the popular award-winning sitcom *The Big Bang Theory.*

As Eileen Pollack points out in her 2013 *New York Times* article "Why Are There Still So Few Women in Science?," *The Big Bang Theory* provides some striking examples of the stereotypes facing women in scientific careers. Unlike Bialik, her character Amy Farrah Fowler is dowdy and socially awkward, standing in stark contrast to Penny, the aspiring actress played by Kaley Cuoco. The universe of the sitcom seems unable to picture a woman who is gifted in both science and show business. The real world, however, proves that this stereotype is wrong, as Bialik has been successful in both of these areas. This disparity between stereotype and reality is a perfect illustration of some of the misconceptions regarding women in the STEM fields.

"STEM" is a shorthand term referring to careers in science, technology, engineering, and mathematics. Statistics reveal a staggering shortage of women in these fields. For instance, as Pollack points out, only

Mayim Bialik's success in both the sciences and show business defies many of the stereotypes that often deter women from the STEM fields. Here, Bialik addresses the National Science Teachers Association.

one-fifth of physics Ph.D.'s in the United States are awarded to women. There are a number of theories and opinions about the causes of this shortage, but it seems obvious that it is due in large part to social conditioning, lack of support, and outright prejudice that women face regarding STEM.

While the difficulties facing women who pursue higher education and careers in scientific fields are well documented, those difficulties should not deter young women who have natural interests and abilities in science. On the contrary, these difficulties illustrate that increasing the number of women in these fields is essential. As more and more women become visible and successful in these fields, the outdated stereotypes surrounding women in science will naturally fall away.

If you are one of the millions of young women with an interest in science and a natural curiosity about the fundamental questions of how the world works, the following information is for you. This resource will explore several career paths that incorporate these skills and interests and will profile female role models who have made achievements in different areas of science. It will also address obstacles facing women in science and the skills, resources, and support networks that will help you prepare for and overcome these obstacles. As a woman with an interest in science, you have an important role to play in helping humanity move forward. Use this information as a resource to help you turn your interests into a rewarding and influential career!

Chapter one

PLANTING SEEDS: EARLY CAREER PREPARATION

What do you picture when you think of a career in science? For many people, the idea might conjure up images of working in a laboratory with test tubes, beakers, white lab coats, and goggles. While there are certainly some careers that involve that kind of work, an interest in science, technology, and/or the natural world can lead to a wide array of jobs. A love of science could lead you to work with animals as a veterinarian or zookeeper or to work with people as a doctor, psychologist, or teacher. You might work as an architect developing more energy-efficient buildings, or you might study the effects of climate change on the ocean and marine life. You might become an author who writes about science in a way that makes it more accessible to people who don't understand it. You might help develop better and more sustainable methods of living on Earth, or you might travel to outer space! The possibilities are numerous and often very different from one another.

Scientist Sheila Sloman works with a rosette, which gathers water samples from various ocean depths to study climate change. Studying climate change is one of many exciting possibilities for women in STEM.

CLASSWORK AND AFTER-SCHOOL CLUBS

While you may not choose a long-term career until college (or even after that), it is never too early to start planning, preparing, and narrowing down your area of focus. Knowing that you are interested in science and nature can play an important role in helping you do that while you are still in high school or even middle school. If you think you may want to pursue a career in science, it is important to take your school's science and math classes seriously. They will lay the foundation for your scientific knowledge and will connect you to the work that you want to do in the future.

Science classes teach you fascinating things about the natural world. A lesson in biology class could spark your interest in a marine biology career. A chemistry lesson could lead you to an exploration of food science. A health class could open your eyes to the importance of teaching proper nutrition and physical fitness.

Math classes help you learn how to think in a logical manner, which is extremely important for any scientific career. Oftentimes, because of negative

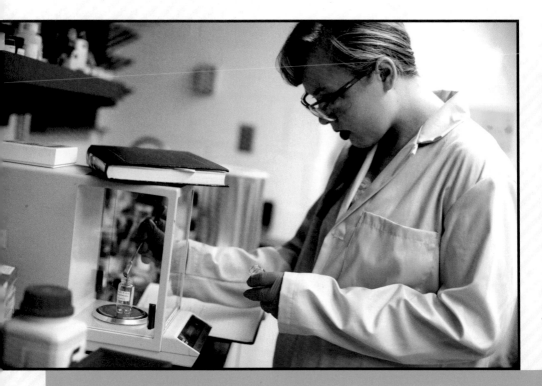

Summer science programs, such as Project SEED at the University of Notre Dame, can provide excellent opportunities for girls to nurture their interest in STEM. Project SEED exposes disadvantaged high school students to the sciences.

stereotypes and inaccurate perceptions that boys are better at math, girls do not pursue math at higher levels. However, these stereotypes should not deter you from trying to excel in math, especially if you enjoy it. The earlier you begin to dedicate serious attention to math classes, and the higher you go in your studies, the more doors you will open for yourself in the future.

In addition to the classes you take during school hours, you can also begin to nurture your interest in science through extracurricular activities. Joining science clubs and entering science fairs or contests can be a great way to make connections with like-minded people.

SMITH COLLEGE SUMMER SCIENCE AND ENGINEERING PROGRAM

Smith College, one of the most prestigious colleges for women in the United States, offers a four-week Summer Science and Engineering Program. It is open to girls, both in the United States and internationally, who are entering grades nine through twelve. Students applying for the program must have demonstrated high academic achievement, but no prior advanced science studies are necessary. Need-based financial aid is available to help with the cost of the program. In past years, more than half of the participants have received financial assistance covering some or all of the tuition cost.

In the four-week program, girls choose two different research courses to attend, each lasting two weeks. The courses cover an eclectic range of topics related to science and engineering. For example, the choices in previous years have included courses such as the Chemistry of Herbal Medicine: A Complex Molecular Story, Narrative and Imagination in Science: A Workshop for Writers, and Designing Intelligent Robots. Smith College faculty members teach the courses, assisted by undergraduate interns. Students do some individual work, but they work mostly in teams to develop research questions and conduct experiments in the field. At the end of each course, students give oral presentations, attended by friends and family, discussing their findings. During weekends and free time, students can use all of the facilities on campus, such as the gyms, libraries, and museums, and they can participate in organized activities like crafts, movies, and talent shows!

Like many other science summer programs for girls, the Smith College program provides an opportunity to develop critical thinking skills, use sophisticated equipment, and learn about discourse (that is, the language used in the field) and scientific procedures. Perhaps more importantly, though, it creates a sense of community and shared purpose among the girls who attend and provides them with mentors and role models.

If you are a high school–aged young woman with an interest in STEM, consider applying to a science summer camp for girls. Not only will you have a fun and interesting summer, you will also meet other girls who share your passion for science. You will have a chance to explore science and technology in greater depth, and you just might discover the topic or question that will lead to your future career!

SUMMER PROGRAMS

Summer programs and camps can be even more intensive ways to pursue an interest in science. There are lots of programs, contests, and camps out there, and many focus specifically on girls in STEM. These programs provide valuable opportunities to explore your specialized interests in more depth than you are able to during the school year, when you have all of your other core subjects to grapple with as well. For science- and technology-minded girls, summer programs can be especially

Learning to network and work together is essential for women in any field, and especially in STEM. Summer programs and after-school clubs foster connection and collaboration.

important, as they allow you to meet and network with other girls who love these subjects enough to spend their summers learning more about them.

Summer programs not only enhance your academic knowledge, but they also help show you that you are a part of a community. This is one of the great things about being a girl who is interested in science: because of the shortage of women in STEM fields, there is a lot of action being taken to change it. As part of your career preparation, you can and should begin to access the programs, scholarships, and other forms of assistance available to young women in STEM. You should also begin to explore your place in the community of women in science, making an effort to meet girls who share your interests and women who are working in the field.

MAKING CONNECTIONS WITH PEOPLE

Science is not always a solitary activity conducted inside a laboratory. There are many careers that combine science and working with people. In this section, we will explore some of those careers and the various levels of education necessary to achieve them. You will find references to four different general types of college degrees: associate's, bachelor's, master's, and doctorate. Although these numbers can vary depending on factors such as the number of courses you take in a semester and whether or not you attend summer classes, an associate's degree requires two years of higher education, a bachelor's degree requires four years, a master's requires six years, and a doctorate requires eight years or more.

CAREERS IN THE MEDICAL FIELD

The first career that comes to mind when most people think about the medical field is that of a doctor. Being a doctor is definitely a respectable, worthwhile, and

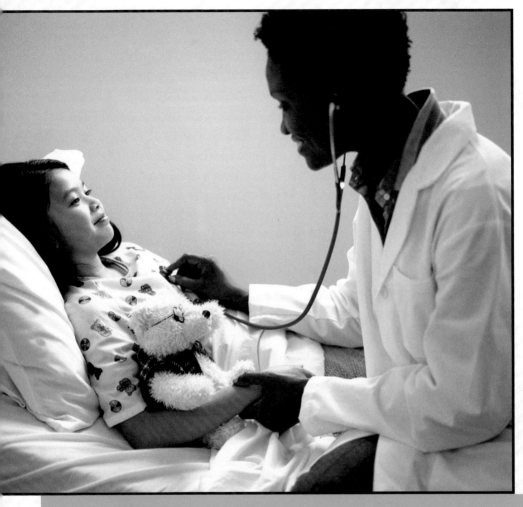

Although it requires a long-term commitment and extensive education, becoming a doctor is one of the most rewarding careers in the sciences. Doctors save and improve lives, and they also make strong connections with patients.

lucrative career, but it also requires a long-term commitment. Earning a doctorate of medicine requires many years of schooling, as well as several years working as a resident. There are many different types of medical doctors, with different specializations, but the education requirements for each are similar. First, you need to get a bachelor's degree. Some colleges offer pre-med programs, but there is no specific major required in order to apply to medical school. It is important, however, to take several science courses. Before applying to medical school, you will need to take the Medical College Admissions Test (MCAT). If you pass the MCAT, you can apply to medical school, which is a four-year program. Following med school, you will complete a three- to seven-year residency. Then, you will take the U.S. Medical Licensing Exam. If you pass the exam, you will be licensed and legally authorized to practice medicine.

Nursing is another medical career in high demand; it requires less schooling than becoming a doctor and often offers more personal interaction with patients. There are a few different educational routes that you can take to become a nurse. The lowest level of nursing certification is licensed practical nurse (LPN), which does not require a degree. LPNs are not registered nurses and are not eligible to work as nurses in hospitals or clinics, but they may work in nursing homes and a few other settings with limited responsibilities. An associate's degree in nursing, or ADN, is the minimum degree required to become a registered nurse. Although those holding ADNs are technically fully qualified nurses, many employers, especially hospitals, require the majority of their nurses to hold BSNs, which are bachelor of science degrees in nursing. Both ADNs and BSNs require clinical experience, but an ADN requires only two years of college while a BSN requires four. You can also earn a master's degree and even a doctorate degree in nursing.

DR. BARBARA ROSS-LEE

The first African American female dean of a U.S. medical school, Dr. Barbara Ross-Lee is a trailblazer for women in the sciences. During her childhood in Detroit, Michigan, Ross-Lee had interests in both the sciences and the arts, and she performed with her sister Diana in their church choir. In the 1960s, as the civil rights movement marched forward, she decided to take her scientific interests to a higher academic level, entering a pre-medicine program at Detroit's Wayne State University with the goal of becoming a doctor. At Wayne State, she faced discrimination from her academic advisor, who,

(continued on the next page)

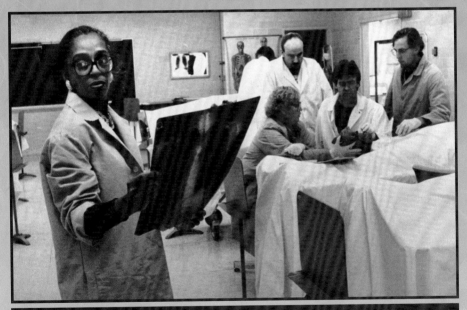

Despite facing many obstacles as an African American woman in the sciences, Dr. Barbara Ross-Lee persevered, becoming the first black woman to be the head of a United States medical school.

(continued from the previous page)

though a woman herself, did not believe women should be medical doctors. The advisor refused to approve human anatomy as Ross-Lee's major. Because of the advisor's refusal, Ross-Lee earned her bachelor's degree in biology and chemistry, which would not allow her to become a doctor.

In the 1960s, teaching was one of the few professions in which women were culturally accepted, so Ross-Lee entered the National Teacher Corps (NTC), a federal program in which she could teach in Detroit public schools while earning a master's degree in teaching. She completed the NTC program in 1969. Shortly after, she found an opportunity to return to her original dream of being a doctor when Michigan State University opened a school of osteopathic medicine in the Detroit suburb of Pontiac. At this point, Ross-Lee was divorced from her first husband and was a single mother. Her determination to become a doctor was so great that she moved back in with her own mother, who could provide child care while Ross-Lee pursued her studies.

Ross-Lee earned her doctorate of osteopathy from Michigan State University in 1973. For ten years, she ran a private family practice in Detroit. In 1984, she was able to combine her two professions by becoming a consultant on education in the health professions for the U.S. Department of Health and Human Services. In 1993, she was appointed dean of the College of Osteopathic Medicine at Ohio University, earning her the distinction as the first African American woman to be the dean of a medical school. During her time at Ohio University, Ross-Lee revamped the College of Osteopathic Medicine's program. Instead of the traditional model of students sitting in a classroom while professors lectured, she introduced a student-centered, problem-solving approach to curriculum, which encouraged students to use their own unique backgrounds and cultural perspectives to change and influence the medical profession and improve health in their communities.

In 2001, Ross-Lee moved on to the New York Institute of Technology, where she became dean of the College of Osteopathic Medicine and vice president of Health Sciences and Medical Affairs. Dr. Barbara Ross-Lee's career proves that women can overcome numerous barriers and have successful, progressive careers in the sciences that combine their talents and improve the lives of the people around them.

MENTAL HEALTH CAREERS

As the stigma surrounding mental health problems is fading, and as mental health issues are becoming more visible, the number of people seeking treatment for and assistance with mental and emotional problems continues to grow. While some mental health professionals, such as social workers and community counselors, may not have a great deal of scientific training, psychologists and psychiatrists do. A psychologist holds a doctorate in psychology (the scientific study of the mind, emotions, and behaviors), while a psychiatrist holds a degree in medicine. Because a psychiatrist is a medical doctor, she can prescribe medicine to patients.

A psychologist provides mental therapy and may sometimes refer patients to a psychiatrist for prescriptions, but she does not write prescriptions. Because a doctorate in psychology does not require medical school or a medical residency, it takes less time to earn than a degree in psychiatry. The

Becoming a math or science teacher can be a wonderful way to share your love of your subject. Teaching provides a unique opportunity to spark students' lifelong interest in STEM.

trade-off, logically, is that psychiatrists generally make more money than psychologists, although both draw fairly high salaries.

CAREERS IN SCIENCE EDUCATION

Another way to work in science and spend time with people is to become an educator. As a student, you know firsthand the influence that a teacher can have on your interest in a subject. Whether or not your science teachers nurture and encourage your interest can play a huge role in your decisions about your future. It is extremely important and beneficial for young women to have role models in the sciences; often, the first role models they encounter are their teachers. As a female science teacher, you would have the opportunity to encourage other young women to continue in the field.

Teaching requires varying levels of education, depending on the level of schooling you want to teach. Elementary school teachers generally teach all subjects, including science, to their students. You can begin a career in elementary education with a bachelor's degree and an elementary-level teaching certification for your state. Most states require teachers to earn a master's degree within a certain period of time after they begin teaching. Teaching secondary (middle and high school) science requires the same. The difference is that secondary-level science teachers generally teach only science, although they may teach different sciences, such as chemistry, biology, and physics. Teaching science at the college level requires more education. Although some universities will hire people with master's degrees as adjunct professors, a doctorate is required to become a full professor with tenure (meaning your job is secure).

Chapter three

NOURISHING AND SUSTAINING

While lots of scientific careers involve working with people themselves, many of these careers also involve working with the food people eat. If you love science, you probably love to break down processes and substances into smaller steps and parts, finding out how things work and what makes them the way they are. In modern times, particularly in developed countries, we have become separated from the processes in which our food reaches us. Often, we do not know any details about where our food comes from or even what, exactly, it contains. An interest in science could lead to a career in which you figure these things out and educate others about them, working as a nutritionist/dietician, food scientist, or farmer.

CAREERS IN NUTRITION

There are different capacities in which a person can work with diet and nutrition, each requiring different certifications and levels of education and expertise.

These classifications and their required preparations vary by country. In the United States, the Academy of Nutrition and Dietetics recognizes two levels of certification for dieticians: an RD (registered dietician) and a DTR (dietetic technician, registered). An RD must have a bachelor's degree from an accredited university and have completed a minimum of 1,200 hours of supervised fieldwork (which is like an internship or student teaching) in an accredited program. In addition to the coursework and fieldwork, the RD must pass the national examination given by the Commission on Dietetic Registration. A DTR must also pass a national examination but can have an associate's degree rather than a bachelor's. DTR certification requires only 450 hours of supervised fieldwork, as opposed to the 1,200 required to become an RD. A career in nutrition can be a wonderful way to educate individuals and the community about how to eat foods that nourish and improve health, as opposed to foods that are harmful.

CAREERS IN FOOD SCIENCE

While RDs and DTRs work directly with people, advising them about their personal diets, people who hold degrees in food science and food technology work with food itself and the laws that govern how food can be grown, prepared, packaged, marketed, and sold. They become flavor chemists, food safety inspectors, packaging specialists, research scientists, and public health officials, among many other things.

Many colleges and universities offer undergraduate and graduate programs in food science. Some of the most prestigious programs are at Cornell

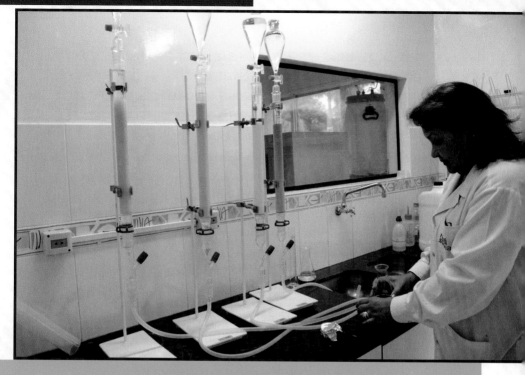

Food scientists inspect our food for quality and safety, and also work to develop new products. The woman pictured here is working on quality control of stevia, a recently developed natural sweetener.

University, Purdue University, Ohio State, and University of Idaho/Washington State University. The Chicago-based Institute for Food Technology (IFT) offers a Certification in Food Science (CFS), which you can earn by completing a bachelor's degree in food science at an approved university. Or you can complete a master's or doctorate in a related field, such as medicine, agricultural science, or biology, and then pass the IFT's certification exam, which is given twice a year.

While all jobs in food science may not require a CFS, it will certainly make any degree that you hold more marketable, and it will make you a more desirable candidate for employment. With a career in food science, you have a chance to influence the way that food is made and processed. By helping determine the standards that govern the safety and quality of food that is sold to the public, you could have a positive effect on the health of the current population and generations to come.

MAKING FEMALE FARMERS VISIBLE

One of the most important steps we can take in changing stereotypes is to increase the visibility of people who prove those stereotypes to be untrue. When most people think of farmers, they picture old white men resembling the Old Macdonald immortalized in the children's song. However, in reality, there are female farmers of all races and ethnicities all over the world. In the United States alone, there are roughly eight thousand farms operated by women. Recently, some photographers have been working on projects that depict female farmers in their everyday activities, showing that the stereotype of the white male farmer is outdated and inaccurate.

One of these projects, simply called the Female Farmer Project, is operated by Audra Mulkern, a self-taught photographer. The project was born when Mulkern started frequenting her local farmer's market and taking pictures of the produce with her phone's camera, eventually self-publishing a photo book. In the course of photographing the food, Mulkern began to build relationships with the farmers themselves. One day, she snapped

(continued on the next page)

(continued from the previous page)

a picture of Sara Cassidy working on Oxbow Farm in Carnation, Washington. The photo inspired Mulkern to purchase and learn to use a better-quality camera, and the Female Farmer Project was born. Describing her philosophy for the project, she told Seedstock.com, "In this country, there is a huge discrepancy in the public mind of what a farmer looks like. A search on images, whether through books or online search engines, reveals very little imagery for women farmers." Through sharing her project online, Mulkern is correcting that discrepancy.

Another photographer, Marji Guyler-Alaniz, shares Mulkern's mission. Guyler-Alaniz's project, FarmHer, displays an online photo gallery of each female farmer she profiles, following each woman through her daily routine. Guyler-Alaniz told the *Huffington Post*, "As a person that grew up in a small town in Iowa, I knew that women are involved in all aspects of agriculture, and always have been an important part of our agricultural system. It hit me that I could change [the popular idea of what a woman farmer looks like] by using my photography to start updating the image of a farmer to include women." With these fascinating and beautiful photo projects, Audra Mulkern and Marji Guyler-Alaniz are making female farmers more visible and therefore are helping change the public's idea of what a farmer looks like.

CAREERS IN AGRICULTURE

Farmers and gardeners work more closely and tangibly with food than those in almost any other profession, especially when you consider that they are in contact with food at its very sources and beginnings. One of the coolest things about a career in farming or gardening

Farming and gardening allow you to work directly with the earth and the plants that you cultivate. Careers in gardening and agriculture lend themselves to entrepreneurship and do not necessarily require higher education.

is that it does not necessarily require any higher education. While a degree in agricultural science or botany would definitely be beneficial to farming and/or gardening, it is not required. You could begin growing food today by taking some seeds and planting them in the soil in your backyard.

Farming and gardening provide excellent opportunities for entrepreneurship—that is, creating your own business and supporting yourself, rather than working for a paycheck from an employer. Of course, in order to do this, you need outside space in which to grow your food and/or keep your animals, as well as money to buy the products and resources you need. For tax purposes, it is generally a good idea to incorporate your business, which makes it a separate entity with a different tax ID from your personal one. There are also several certifications that farmers can earn, which may make their products more marketable, such as USDA Organic certification and Farm Animal Welfare certification from the American Humane Society. You do not have to live on a farm, or even in the country, to pursue this type of career. If you live in the city and are serious about farming and gardening, you should begin volunteering at a community garden or an urban farm, join a club such as the 4-H Club or the Future Farmers of America, and/or start experimenting with growing food in your own backyard.

ALL CREATURES GREAT AND SMALL

While some people love working with humans, others prefer the company of animals. Were you the type of child who played with worms or noticed every squirrel that crossed your path? If this sounds like you, then you might be interested in a career working with animals.

CAREERS IN VETERINARY MEDICINE

This is one of the first careers that will come to most people's minds when they think of working with animals. You may be surprised to learn that veterinarians, just like medical doctors for humans, must earn a bachelor's degree (preferably in biology or one of the other physical sciences) and then obtain a doctorate degree from a veterinary school. Furthermore, there are far fewer veterinary schools than there are medical schools, so admissions to veterinary schools may be more competitive. However, you can complete veterinary school within four years, without doing the residency required to be-

Veterinarians and vet techs work not only in offices and clinics but also in zoos, in animal shelters, or on farms, like the vet seen here examining a pig in its stable.

come an medical doctor. You simply have to complete an accredited program and fulfill the licensing requirements for your state, including passing the North American Veterinary Licensing Exam.

If you want to work in veterinary medicine but do not want to become a fully licensed veterinarian, you might consider becoming a veterinary technician. Becoming a vet tech requires only a two-year or four-year program, as opposed to the additional years required for veterinary school. Veterinary technicians work in various settings, such as zoos, veterinary clinics, and animal shelters.

JANE GOODALL

As a child, Jane Goodall relished books about animals, such as the Doctor Dolittle and Tarzan series, and she began to dream of living among animals in the wild and documenting what she learned. As the Jane Goodall Institute's website notes, "African wildlife adventures were an unlikely calling for a little girl in the 1930s and 1940s." However, as the site goes on to point out, her mother was very supportive of her dream and told her that she could accomplish anything she set out to do.

When Goodall was twenty-two, a friend invited her to visit her family's farm in Kenya. At the time, Goodall was working as a film studio assistant in London and did not have the money to make the trip. She quickly moved back home to the town of Bournemouth and began to save for the journey, recognizing that this was her opportunity to pursue her dream. Goodall finally arrived in Mombasa, Kenya, in 1957. While in Kenya, she met Louis Leakey, a well-known paleontologist/archaeologist. Leakey hired her as his assistant and eventually asked her to observe a group of wild chimpanzees living on the beach at Gombe in Tanzania (then known as Tanganyika), reasoning that the study of chimpanzee life could lead to a greater understanding of evolution.

In 1960, Goodall set foot on the Gombe beach and began living her dream of observing and writing about wildlife. It took time for her to find an effective method of observation, as the chimps were shy and ran from her whenever she got close. Eventually, however, she found a spot on a mountain peak where she could watch the chimps through binoculars.

(continued on the next page)

Jane Goodall's studies of chimpanzees in Tanzania were incredibly influential in the fields of science and anthropology. Her work led to a deeper understanding of the chimps' behavior and its relationship to human behavior.

(continued from the previous page)

Through her observations, Goodall learned many things about chimpanzees that humans up until then did not know. She saw the chimps using tools to catch termites for food; until that point, humans were thought to be the only animals capable of using tools. She discovered that chimpanzees were not vegetarian, as had been previously thought, but that they sometimes ate meat, including other monkeys. At times, the chimps could be just as brutal and aggressive as humans, fighting for status within their own group and warring with rival groups. But she also learned that they were just as capable of compassion as humans are when she observed two adolescent male chimps adopting and protecting abandoned chimps.

Goodall's work challenged humanity's view of itself as the only species with social intelligence and the use of technology. In addition to her observational work, Goodall has worked through the Jane Goodall Institute on ecological efforts to preserve the chimpanzees and their environment, as well as humanitarian efforts to assist the people who live in nearby areas. She also started Roots & Shoots, a humanitarian/environmental organization for youth with members from 130 different countries. Jane Goodall's early interest in animals led to a world-changing career in the sciences.

CAREERS IN ZOOLOGY

A zoologist is someone who studies animals, both in their natural environments and in laboratories. Zoologists study the origins and development of different species, as well as animals' behaviors and interactions with each other, their environments, and other animals. Becoming a zoologist requires a minimum of a bachelor's degree, but zoology studies can be continued at the master's and doctorate levels as well.

Zoologists perform many different kinds of jobs. Some work as zookeepers, monitoring the environments and behaviors of zoo animals, feeding them, and giving tours and educational presentations to visitors. Some zoologists work as wildlife educators at various locations, such as parks or wildlife preserves. Their duties include researching and writing information for print materials and websites, planning and

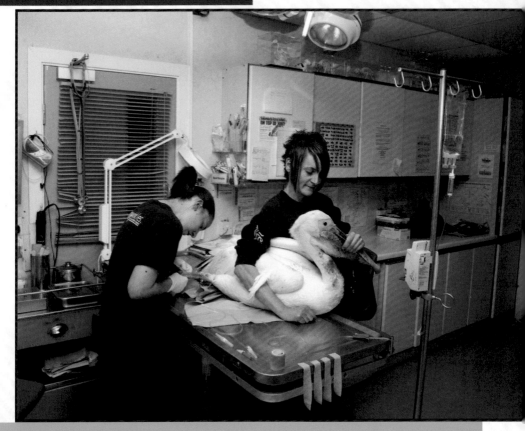

One of the most rewarding things that zoologists do is to care for and rehabilitate injured animals and return them to their habitats. Here, two nurses treat a great white pelican.

giving presentations, designing displays, and raising or buying animals to be exhibited. Some zoologists also work as researchers, conducting experiments and observations both in laboratories and in the field to help solve health issues and environmental problems. Others work as wildlife rehabilitators, caring for injured, sick, and orphaned wildlife and helping return the animals to their habitats.

While some zoologists study a broad range of species, some may specialize in the study of a particular species, such as birds (ornithology) or amphibians (herpetology). Some might focus on the study of fish (ichthyology) or creatures that live specifically in oceans and other bodies of saltwater (marine biology). Because it is closely related to oceanography, the section on environmental careers will discuss marine biology in a bit more detail.

Like Jane Goodall, some scientists who work with animals may become writers, documenting their experiences and findings. Most zoologists who conduct research will publish in academic journals. However, some, like Goodall, choose to translate their writings into language that people outside of the field can grasp and understand. Becoming a zoological writer could be combined with research or other fieldwork.

If you think you might want to pursue a career working with animals, you should explore the possibility of volunteering at a wildlife preserve, an animal shelter, or a zoo. Whether you are interested in veterinary medicine, caring for injured wildlife, or simply studying animals in their natural environments, volunteering is a valuable way to get started. Direct hands-on experience will look fantastic on college applications, and volunteering can help you build your network.

OUR CHANGING EARTH

Animals are an important part of the world around us, but they (and we) could not exist without the life-sustaining environment on the planet. For many years now, scientists have been telling us that our environment is changing and that many of those changes are the result of our own actions as a human race. There have always been careers in which people study the natural environment, such as the ocean, the atmosphere, and the earth's core. Given our current knowledge about the ways that we have changed and are changing the environment, these jobs are taking on even greater importance.

CAREERS IN CLIMATOLOGY AND GEOLOGY

Climatology is the study of weather and its patterns and changes. This study is done through hands-on research. The research conducted by climatologists is used in weather forecasting, agricultural planning, and

Geologists often work in the field to study the effects of drilling beneath the earth's surface for oil. This scientist is collecting samples from caves in Malaysia.

the designs of buildings, among other things. Climatologists may work in universities, private agencies, or branches of federal, state, or local government. They often split their time between working in the office and working out in the field, collecting samples from soil, air, water, ice cores, and plant life.

The minimum level of education required to become a climatologist is a bachelor's degree. At the bachelor's level, climatology is usually combined with meteorology (the study of weather forecasting). In order to teach at a college or obtain a prestigious research position, you will need a master's or a doctorate, which means conducting an original research project and writing up the results in a dissertation.

Geologists study the earth itself, the rocks it is made of, and how those rocks have changed and continue to change. Like climatologists, geologists may work in universities, for government agencies, or for private companies. For example, gas companies may employ geologists to study the effects of drilling for oil, and government agencies may consult geologists when developing policies regarding such drilling. While private companies may hire someone with a bachelor's degree in geology or earth science, most government agencies will want geologists with graduate degrees, which are also necessary for teaching geology at the university level.

CAREERS IN OCEANOGRAPHY AND MARINE BIOLOGY

Marine biologists study the living creatures in bodies of water, including oceans. Like climatologists, they are sometimes employed by government agencies. With a bachelor's degree in marine biology, you might find an entry-level job, for instance working with the Bureau of Land Management or the National Park Service. Research positions will generally require a higher level of degree, such as a master's or doctorate. Marine biologists also work for aquariums, environmental organizations, and schools. They almost always spend some of their work time traveling, as they often need to conduct field research in a wide range of marine environments.

Oceanographer Dr. Sylvia Earle works with another diver to document the fish population in the Florida Keys National Marine Sanctuary as a part of the Great American Fish Count.

While a marine biologist studies creatures that live in the ocean, an oceanographer studies the ocean itself. There are several types of oceanographers. Biological oceanographers do work similar to that of marine biologists, studying living organisms. Physical oceanographers study the tides, waves, and currents. Chemical oceanographers study the chemical composition of the ocean, and geological oceanographers study the ocean floor. As our oceans change due to natural shifts, global warming, and other phenomena created by humans, such as oil spills, the work of oceanographers is becoming more crucial. According to the Bureau of Labor Statistics, the number of jobs available in this field is expected to grow by 21 percent between 2012 and 2022.

RACHEL CARSON

Born in 1907 in the rural town of Springdale, Pennsylvania, Rachel Carson transformed her early love of the natural world into a career that combined science, writing, and activism. Carson's passion for the natural world was inherited from her mother and fed by her explorations of the family's farm and the nearby river. She began to express her interest in nature through writing at the early age of eight, when she started penning short stories that often included animals. She was also an avid reader, favoring authors such as Beatrix Potter, Herman Melville, and Robert Louis Stevenson, whose works portray the natural world, particularly animals and the sea.

Carson completed her undergraduate studies at Pennsylvania College for Women, where she continued to write but began to focus more heavily on her scientific interests, eventually

(continued on page 42)

Writer, activist, and scientist Rachel Carson launched the environmental/ecological movement as we know it today. She did extensive work to raise awareness of the effects that human actions have on the natural environment.

(continued from page 40)

switching her major from English to marine biology. In 1932, she earned a master's degree in zoology from Johns Hopkins University. She worked as a radio scriptwriter for the U.S. Department of Fisheries and wrote natural history articles for the *Baltimore Sun*. In 1936, she became editor in chief of all the U.S. Fish and Wildlife Service's publications.

While she supported herself through this scientific writing, Carson continued to work on her own more lyrical nature writing in her free time. This work led to her award-winning books about the ocean, *The Sea Around Us* and *Edge of the Sea*. These books were not written for a scientific audience but for the general public. Carson was sharing her love of and knowledge about the sea with readers who did not have advanced scientific training. Following the success of these books, she retired from her governmental work in order to focus on this writing, which was her true passion.

In 1962, Rachel Carson published *Silent Spring*, her most famous work. This book questioned and challenged the practices of the U.S. government and agricultural scientists, particularly the practice of using chemical pesticides. *Silent Spring* asked humans to change their view of the natural environment and their position in it, to live more harmoniously with the rest of nature instead of harming the environment through domination. Carson and *Silent Spring* helped begin the ecological/environmental movement as we know it today.

Carson died from breast cancer in 1964, a year after she testified at a congressional hearing about human health and the environment. Her life and her work continue to inspire new generations of women with a passion for science and the environment. One of these women is Sylvia Earle, an author and oceanographer who serves as explorer in residence for National Geographic.

Climatology, geology, marine biology, and ocean-ography are just a few of the scientific careers involving the natural environment. Other careers, such as environmental engineering, architecture, and urban planning, can use scientific research to help create more sustainable ways of living. As we continue to observe, discover, and cope with the ways that our environment is changing, the demand for these careers is sure to grow, and new career opportunities are sure to develop.

"TO INFINITY AND BEYOND

A s important as it is to study and explore humanity and the planet we live on, there are also many career opportunities involving exploration of the world beyond Earth: that is, outer space. Ask any group of children what they want to be when they grow up, and chances are at least one or two will say they want to be an astronaut. However, many people are unclear about how one might become an astronaut. When we watch cartoon astronaut Buzz Lightyear in the *Toy Story* movies, wanting to be an astronaut seems almost make-believe, like wanting to be a pirate or a princess when you grow up. Becoming an astronaut, however, is entirely possible. There are also many other careers involving the study of outer space and the development of equipment to assist in that study.

BECOMING AN ASTRONAUT

While many scientific careers can lead to jobs in different companies and settings, being an astronaut means working for one entity in particular: the National Aeronautics and Space Administration, or NASA. As

Space travel is one of the most exciting career possibilities for women in STEM. Here, astronaut Sunita Williams is outfitted in a space suit in preparation for a walk in space.

NASA's website points out, the word "astronaut" derives from Greek words that mean "space sailor." In modern times, the word refers exclusively to "space sailors" from the United States; people who go to outer space in the Russian space program, for example, are called "cosmonauts."

In order to be eligible to be an astronaut, you must have a bachelor's degree in biological science, physical science, engineering, or mathematics. You also need at least three years of professional experience or one thousand hours of time spent as pilot in command of a jet aircraft. If you have a higher degree, you do not need to have as many years of professional experience. NASA encourages educators, including K–12 teachers as well as professors, to apply. There are physical requirements for astronauts as well, including near 20/20 vision, blood pressure at or below 140/90, and height between 62 and 75 inches (157 and 190 centimeters). Astronaut candidates must also pass NASA's physical exam.

These requirements make you eligible to apply to be an astronaut candidate. Being selected as an astronaut candidate does not necessarily mean you will be selected as an astronaut. You must complete all of the training and be evaluated successfully in order to become an astronaut. However, astronaut candidates who are not selected as astronauts are often given other positions within NASA.

SALLY RIDE

Sally Ride was the first U.S. woman to visit outer space. Born in 1951 in Encino, California, Ride was interested in science from the time she was a young child. Her parents encouraged her interest, and she owned a telescope and a chemistry set. She also loved sports, especially tennis. She competed in tournaments and was talented enough to win a tennis scholarship to Westlake School for Girls in Los Angeles.

Ride went on to earn degrees in both English and physics from Stanford University by 1977. She was pursuing her doctorate in physics when she learned that NASA was recruiting scientists and engineers to become astronauts. Until that time, astronauts had primarily been military pilots, and all of them had been men. This was the first time women had been allowed to apply. Ride's application was one of eight thousand to be submitted. In 1978, she became one of thirty-five people chosen from those eight thousand; only six of them were women.

Ride spent several years training, and on June 18, 1983, she became the first U.S. woman to soar into outer space on the spaceship *Challenger*. Speaking of that mission, she said, "The thing that I'll remember most about the flight is that it was fun. In fact, I'm sure it was the most fun I'll ever have in my life." Ride flew into space again in 1984 aboard shuttle STS 41-G. When the *Challenger* exploded in 1986, killing the seven crewmembers aboard, Ride served on the committee that investigated the tragedy. Following that, she took on a leadership role at NASA, eventually becoming director of the Office of Exploration.

After retiring from NASA in 1987, Ride became a professor of physics at the University of California, San Diego and the director of the California Space Institute. In 2001, she and her life partner, Tam O'Shaughnessy, founded Sally Ride Science, a company with the mission of encouraging young people, especially girls, to pursue careers in STEM.

Ride received numerous awards and honors during her lifetime. She passed away in 2012, and in 2013, she was posthumously awarded the Presidential Medal of Freedom. Her legacy continues through Sally Ride Science and the many people she continues to inspire. Dr. Sally Ride opened the doors for women astronauts, paving the way for many others, including Mae C. Jemison, who in 1992 became the first African American woman in space.

ASTRONOMERS, PHYSICISTS, AND AEROSPACE ENGINEERS

While astronauts are the only people whose job involves actual space travel, other jobs involve the study of outer space and the design of equipment used in outer space. Astronomers, physicists, and aerospace engineers all contribute in various ways to make space travel safe and possible.

An astronomer is a person who studies the stars and planets. Astronomers spend a lot of time behind microscopes and working with computers. Using the principles of mathematics and physics, astronomers gather information about stars, planets, moons, and other celestial bodies and objects. Their work includes developing scientific theories, writing research proposals, and analyzing data. A lot of time is spent compiling their research into scientific papers and presenting to colleagues at conferences and in other settings. Almost all astronomers hold Ph.D.'s, and they usually complete an additional two or three years of postdoctoral research.

Physics involves the exploration of motion, matter, and energy, both on Earth and in outer space. People who actually work as physicists, whether professors or researchers, almost always hold a Ph.D. However, a bachelor's or master's degree in physics can provide a good foundation for other scientific careers, particularly in the engineering field.

Aerospace engineers, on the other hand, need only a bachelor's degree to obtain licensure and begin work in their field. Aerospace engineers design aircraft and missiles as well as the spacecraft

Astronauts are not the only scientists involved in space exploration. Aerospace engineers, such as the woman pictured here, design and inspect aircraft, missiles, and spacecraft.

and satellites used in space exploration. They are employed by both private industries and government organizations.

Humans have been exploring outer space from afar for centuries through astronomy and have been exploring it firsthand for many years through space programs. The universe is so vast, however, that we have not even begun to learn all there is to learn and discover out there. If you have an interest in outer space, consider a career in one of these fields. Like Sally Ride and Mae C. Jemison, you, too, could be a pioneering woman in the field of space exploration!

Chapter seven

MAKING IT HAPPEN: BASIC CAREER TIPS

When preparing for a career in science or any other field, there are certain things you need to know: how to conduct an effective job search, develop a résumé, and attend a job interview, for example. The earlier you begin to research and practice these things, the more naturally they will come when it is time to begin conducting a job search. Here you will find some basic tips for career preparation. You should follow these tips any time you are applying for a job, even if it is just an after-school retail job to bring in some extra pocket money. That way, by the time you are ready to apply for your dream job in a STEM field, these things will come as second nature.

CREATING A RÉSUMÉ

No matter what type of career you are seeking, you will definitely need a résumé that is both attention-catching and simple to understand. It is wise to begin compiling a résumé as early as possible in your career. If you have the basic structure in place, you

An important step in career preparation is to begin developing a résumé, which can be edited and supplemented as you gain new skills and experience.

can easily add to it and revise it as you gain more experience.

One important thing to remember about a résumé is that in the overwhelming majority of cases, it gets you the interview, not the job. Hiring managers see many, many résumés come across their desks or into their e-mail in-boxes when they are looking to fill a position. The ones that stand out determine who gets an interview.

Whether or not a résumé stands out is often based on the appearance and organization of the document itself, not just the information it contains.

Career expert Tony Bashara told *Forbes* magazine that including too much information could actually harm your chances of moving on to the interview stage. He says that résumés should be simple and straightforward and that someone with no experience in the field should be able to understand the information you provide. You should find the simplest format possible and use a font that looks professional and is easy to read.

MENTORING

When it comes to career advice, a mentor is one of the most valuable resources you can have. A mentor can help you learn from successes and mistakes before you even make them. For women in STEM fields, having a mentor is even more essential, for many reasons. A mentor can offer personal advice and experiences that can help you prepare for the unique challenges faced by women in STEM. As an article on SciDev.Net phrases it, "Women meet more career barriers in science than men do…Support from mentors can help women overcome these barriers."

There are lots of organizations devoted to connecting women in STEM with mentors. For example, the Massachusetts chapter of the Association for Women in Science organizes mentoring circles, in which one or two mentors are matched with four to five mentees. The circle meets for between two and six hours a month over the course of eight months. Mentors are women who work in the sciences, either in academia or for businesses, and they

(continued on the next page)

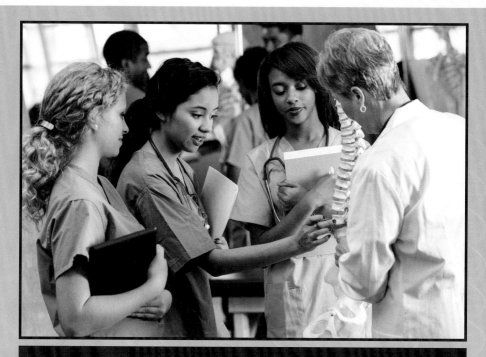

Mentorship is extremely beneficial for women in the sciences. Here, a medical school professor shares her expertise with young nursing students.

(continued from the previous page)

are paired with mentees who have career goals in their areas of expertise. In 2013, a pilot program called Women in Technology Sharing Online, or WitsOn, was launched to connect female students with prominent women in the field. In this program, students and professors submit questions online, and the mentors answer them. Participants in the initial program included the first black female astronaut, Mae C. Jemison, and Jacqueline K. Barton, the chairwoman of the chemistry department at CalTech.

Universities also have mentoring programs for women in the sciences. At Brown University, the WiSE (Women in Science and Engineering) program pairs incoming freshman with a third- or fourth-year mentor who can help guide them through course selections, connect them with resources, and help them learn to work and communicate with professors. Purdue University's Women in Science programs provide support for both undergraduate and graduate students. Through the Residence Program, first-year undergraduates live in a dorm with other students who have similar academic interests. First-years are also paired with mentors from higher classes. The Graduate Mentoring Program consists of a series of dinner meetings at which graduate students and postdoctoral students meet and converse with dedicated female scientists.

INTERVIEWING FOR A JOB

The interview is often the most intimidating and the most important step in the job search process. It is your chance to give an impression of yourself as competent, confident, and enthusiastic about the field and the position to which you are applying. It may be a cliché, but it is also true: first impressions are extremely important.

Even if you think the job you are applying for allows casual dress, you should err on the side of caution for an interview and dress professionally. You should also take some time to prepare. While you cannot know in advance the exact questions you will be asked, you can anticipate the general information you think your interviewer will want to know. Be prepared to discuss your employment history, your strengths and weaknesses, and your future goals in the field. Remember

Job interviews provide the opportunity to create a great first impression. It is essential to dress professionally, project confidence, and appear prepared and knowledgeable about the position for which you are applying.

that when an interviewer asks about your weaknesses, he or she does not usually want a truly self-deprecating answer. Choose a weakness that is also in some ways a strength, such as, "I tend to take on too much and sometimes have trouble asking for help." When asked about your future goals in the field, you want to be honest, but make sure that you convey genuine interest in the job for which you are interviewing. No one is going to hire someone who seems disinterested or thinks she is above the position. If you are interviewing for a part-time or entry-level job that you do not intend to keep forever, stress the ways in which the job contributes to your long-term goals.

FOLLOWING UP

After an interview, it is a good idea to send an e-mail to the people you met. This e-mail should be short and simple, thanking the interviewers for their time and expressing enthusiasm about the next steps in the hiring process. Sending a thank-you e-mail shows grace and professionalism and may help you stand out among other candidates who have been interviewed. Following the thank-you e-mail, you should avoid hounding the company about a decision, although it is a good idea to follow up once or twice. Most companies will inform you quickly if they have decided to hire someone else. However, if a couple of weeks have gone by and you have not heard anything, you can send an e-mail inquiring about the status of your application.

The process of applying for, interviewing for, and obtaining a job is only the beginning. Once you are hired for a job in your field, your career has truly begun. Next, you will find some advice on how you can continue your development and grow as a professional woman in the scientific career you have chosen.

Chapter eight

A LIFETIME OF LEARNING

L ike all professions, careers in science require a lifelong commitment to learning, growth, and professional development. Finding a specific career is only the beginning of this process. As you continue to grow and succeed in your field, you will constantly discover new challenges and new opportunities.

RESEARCH AND WRITING

Any professional, and especially a professional in the sciences, needs to keep abreast of the latest research findings and methodologies in her field. As new information is gained and old theories are updated or discarded, the body of knowledge in any scientific field grows and changes. In order to keep up with the times, you need to read academic journals and magazines that cover your field and related fields. You need to make sure that when new developments occur, you know about them and can discuss them with your colleagues.

Japanese researchers present their findings on a new regenerative procedure to treat age-related macular degeneration. Sharing research findings at conferences is one of the ways that scientists continue their development throughout their careers.

Speaking of colleagues, maintaining a network of professional associates is another important aspect of your lifelong commitment to your scientific career. Support from colleagues is an invaluable resource for women in the sciences. Even after you have spent several years in your profession and may even be mentoring aspiring women yourself, you still need the support that a network of colleagues can provide.

For scientists in academia, publishing one's own research findings is absolutely essential. Sharing your research in the form of academic journal articles

THE PROS AND CONS OF EARNING HIGHER DEGREES

You always have the opportunity to become more educated in your field. Even if your current job or certification requires only an associate's or a bachelor's degree, continuing your education at the graduate level can make you more competent in your current job and can open doors to higher-paying jobs. Even if you have earned the highest possible degree in your specific profession, you could pursue a degree in a related field in order to expand your knowledge. You never know when you might want to enter a different aspect of your profession. Even if you are completely happy in the first job you take in the field and want to remain in that position, it never hurts to learn more.

Of course, most people do not have unlimited finances with which to pursue a large number of degrees. Spending money you can't afford on degrees that will not increase your earning potential can be a bad decision. Realistically, you should consider several factors when deciding whether to take your formal education to a higher level, such as how much money you already owe in student loans, whether or not scholarships or fellowships are available for the program you want to enter, whether the higher degree will increase your earning potential, and whether that increase will balance out any financial hardship a further degree would create. Remember, too, that many companies provide full or partial tuition assistance for employees who want to continue their education. Earning a higher degree may not always be the right choice, but it can sometimes be a wise and fulfilling decision. Although you may not have a complete educational plan in mind right now, it is never too early to start considering and planning this aspect of your professional development.

will be an important part of your professional career. Also, professionals often write books directed at their colleagues in the field that are designed for academic research. However, it shows great skill to be able to write about complicated technical or scientific information in a way that the general public can understand. This type of writing, too, can be a wonderful way to continue your development as a professional in STEM.

COMBATING STEREOTYPE THREAT

The phenomenon of "stereotype threat" was first named by psychologist Claude Steele and his colleagues as they studied the reasons why girls, despite being just as skilled at math as their male counterparts, sometimes did not perform as well. Steele and the psychologists with whom he worked discovered that, across all races, genders, and ethnicities, people's performance in all kinds of activities was hindered when they feared that they might fulfill a negative stereotype. As Shankar Vedantam discusses in the NPR article "How Stereotypes Can Drive Women to Quit Science," stereotype threat is not limited to academic settings. It can and does affect many people's performance in the workplace, and the accompanying stress can discourage women in science, even causing them to leave the field.

Some people criticize the theory of stereotype threat, claiming that it "blames the victim"—implying the problem is all in the head of the person who fears the stereotype. That is certainly not the case. Women are wary of stereotypes (in science and other aspects of life) because they exist and have been used to harm and deter women for many years. The concept of

Due to stereotype threat and lack of confidence, girls sometimes underachieve in science and math classes. Fighting this phenomenon and helping to build young girls' confidence is important for female professionals in STEM.

stereotype threat should not be used to put the blame on women, and it should not deter you as a young woman from pursuing a career in science. Instead, you should use your awareness of this phenomenon to help you understand and cope with some of the difficulties you may face. Eventually, if women continue to break ground in STEM fields and fight the stereotypes that currently exist, those stereotypes will fade from our cultural landscape and will no longer carry any threat. As you continue to grow as a professional, seek the support you need to help you stay strong and persevere in your field.

PROFESSIONAL ORGANIZATIONS AND MENTORING

Joining one or more professional associations can help you stay current on developments in the field and help you build and maintain a network of colleagues. There are lots of organizations for women and girls in scientific fields, such as the Association for Women in Science and the National Girls

Support from female mentors can help young girls fight stereotype threat and excel in science, technology, engineering, and math. Mentoring is one of the most important contributions that professional women in STEM can make.

Collaborative Project. Joining these organizations can help you feel like part of a community and can give you the opportunity to mentor young women in STEM. When you have gone through all of the preparation and educational steps and have finally earned your status as a professional, joining an organization and becoming a mentor will help you reach back, to connect with young women in the future who share the same interests, fears, and aspirations that you have right now. Look forward to that time, when you have come full circle and can help lift up other girls, and let that inspire you to reach for your dreams right now!

DETER To discourage someone from a course of action by instilling fear or apprehension.

DIETETIC TECHNICIAN, REGISTERED (DTR) Dietician who has passed the certification exam but has only completed an associate's degree and the minimum amount of fieldwork.

DISPARITY A very noticeable difference.

ECLECTIC Exhibiting or drawing inspiration from a wide range of interests, styles, subjects, and/or genres.

HERPETOLOGY The study of amphibians.

HUMANITARIAN Promoting the well-being of one's fellow humans.

LICENSED PRACTICAL NURSE (LPN) Nurse who is licensed but does not have a degree and cares for the elderly or convalescent in settings such as nursing homes, under the supervision of doctors and registered nurses.

LUCRATIVE Profitable; earning lots of money.

ORNITHOLOGY The study of birds.

OSTEOPATHY Branch of medicine that treats and heals muscles and joints through moving, stretching, and massaging.

PSYCHIATRIST Mental health practitioner with a doctorate in medicine.

PSYCHOLOGIST Mental health practitioner with a doctorate in psychology.

REGISTERED DIETICIAN (RD) Dietician who has completed a bachelor's degree, completed an increased amount of fieldwork, and passed the examination for certification.

SELF-DEPRECATING Overly modest; belittling oneself, often in an attempt at humor.

STEM Acronym used to refer to careers in science, technology, engineering, and mathematics.

STIGMA Cultural shame or disgrace.

SUSTAINABLE Able to be maintained.

TENURE Job security earned by a teacher or professor after working for a certain amount of time and fulfilling designated requirements.

For More Information

Alberta Women's Science Network (AWSN)
Box 349, 305-4625 Varsity Drive NW
Calgary, AB T3A 0Z9
Canada
(403) 616-4474
Website: http://www.awsn.com
Alberta Women's Science Network strives to
recruit, retain, and recognize women in the
sciences. Through its mentoring program, it
works to encourage youth, especially girls, to
pursue careers in science.

American Medical Women's Association (AMWA)
12100 Sunset Hills Road, Suite 130
Reston, VA 20190
(703) 234-4069
Website: http://www.amwa-doc.org
Founded in 1915 by Dr. Barbara VanHoosen,
AMWA has been working to encourage and
support women in medicine and to improve
women's health. It does this through education, advocacy, mentoring, and building
networks and alliances.

Canadian Association for Girls in Science (CAGIS)
6519-B Mississauga Road
Mississauga, ON L5N 1A6
Canada
(905) 567-7190
Website: http://www.cagis.ca
Inspired by a nine-year-old girl named Larissa
Vingilis-Jeremko, CAGIS is a network of girls

ages seven to sixteen who love science. They meet monthly to participate in hands-on activities led by professionals from many different fields. The club is led by the girls themselves, who write their own newsletter and magazine and plan their own events.

Center for STEM Education for Girls
The Harpeth Hall School
3801 Hobbes Road
Nashville, TN 37215
(615) 297-0480
Website: http://www.stemefg.org
The Center for STEM Education for Girls draws together elementary, secondary, and university-level educators for annual meetings to discuss the best practices for educating girls in STEM and find new ways to encourage girls' involvement in STEM. The center hosts a summer conference for teachers with hands-on workshops and a summer STEM institute for ninth- and tenth-grade girls in Tennessee schools.

Jane Goodall's Roots & Shoots
The Jane Goodall Institute
1595 Spring Hill Road, Suite 550
Vienna, VA 22182
(703) 682-9220
Website: http://www.rootsandshoots.org
Roots & Shoots began with a back-porch meeting between Jane Goodall and twelve teenagers

from her community in Tanzania in 1991.
The organization empowers young people all
over the world to find solutions to problems
in their communities through innovation and
collaboration.

National Girls Collaborative Project (NGCP)
3500 188 Street SW, Suite 490
Lynwood, WA 98037
Website: http://www.ngcproject.org
Started in 2002 and funded by the National Science
    Foundation, NGCP works to unite organiza-
    tions that share the vision of encouraging girls
    to excel in science, technology, engineering,
    and math. By bringing different organizations
    together, NGCP helps them share and maximize
    resources. Building a network strengthens each
    individual organization.

Science Club for Girls (SCFG)
Congregation Eitz Chayim
136 Magazine Street
Cambridge, MA 02139
Website: http://scienceclubforgirls.org
By offering free programming with a fun, inter-
    active approach to science, SCFG connects
    young women, especially those from under-
    represented groups, with female mentors in
    STEM. The girls who participate in the men-
    toring program eventually take on leadership
    roles of their own, working to nurture younger
    girls with scientific interests.

Women, Food and Agriculture Network (WFAN)
P.O. Box 611
Ames, IA 50010
(515) 460-2477
Website: http://www.wfan.org
WFAN is a network of women involved in sustainable agriculture. The organization works to share information and empower women to help create healthy, sustainable, environmentally sound food systems in their communities.

WEBSITES

Because of the changing nature of Internet links, Rosen Publishing has developed an online list of websites related to the subject of this book. This site is updated regularly. Please use this link to access the list:

http://www.rosenlinks.com/TECH/Sci

For Further Reading

Aubrey, Sarah Beth. *The Profitable Hobby Farm: How to Build a Sustainable Local Foods Business.* Hoboken, NJ: Howell Book House, 2010.

Carson, Rachel. *Silent Spring.* New York, NY: Houghton Mifflin, 2002.

Costa, Temra. *Farmer Jane: Changing the Way We Eat.* Layton, UT: Gibbs Smith, 2010.

Des Jardins, Julie. *The Madam Curie Complex: The Hidden History of Women in Science.* New York, NY: The Feminist Press at CUNY, 2010.

Etingoff, Kim. *Women in Chemistry.* Broomall, PA: Mason Crest, 2013.

Etingoff, Kim. *Women in Medicine.* Broomall, PA: Mason Crest, 2013.

Field, Shelley. *Career Opportunities Working with Animals.* New York, NY: Checkmark Books, 2011.

Gibson, Karen Bush. *Women in Space: 23 Stories of First Flights, Scientific Missions, and Gravity-Breaking Adventures.* Chicago, IL: Chicago Review Press, 2014.

Goodall, Jane. *In the Shadow of Man.* Wilmington, MA: Mariner Books, 2010.

Gornick, Vivian. *Women in Science: Then and Now.* New York, NY: The Feminist Press at CUNY, 2009.

Indovino, Shaina. *Women in the Environmental Sciences.* Broomall, PA: Mason Crest, 2013.

Indovino, Shaina. *Women in Space.* Broomall, PA: Mason Crest, 2013.

Institute for Career Research. *Careers in Nutrition— Dietician, Nutritionist.* Chicago, IL: Institute for Career Research, 2012.

James, Abigail Norfleet. *Teaching the Female Brain: How Girls Learn Math and Science.* Thousand Oaks, CA: Corwin, 2009.

Koch, Janice, Barbara Polnick, and Beverly Irby, eds. *Girls and Women in STEM: A Never Ending Story.* Charlotte, NC: Information Age Publishing, 2013.

Levine, Ellen S. *Up Close: Rachel Carson.* New York, NY: Puffin, 2008.

Prinstein, Michael J. *The Portable Mentor: Expert Guide to a Successful Career in Psychology.* New York, NY: Springer, 2012.

Sherr, Lynn. *Sally Ride: America's First Woman in Space.* New York, NY: Simon & Schuster, 2014.

Shewfelt, Robert L. *Becoming a Food Scientist: To Graduate School and Beyond.* New York, NY: Springer, 2012.

Thistlewaite, Rebecca. *Farms with a Future: Creating and Growing a Sustainable Farm Business.* White River Junction, VT: Chelsea Green Publishing, 2013.

Bibliography

About Bioscience. "Bioscience Careers: Zoologist." Retrieved October 18, 2014 (http://www
.aboutbioscience.org/careers/zoologist).

Academy of Nutrition and Dietetics. "Become an
RD/DTR." Retrieved October 17, 2014 (http://
www.eatright.org/BecomeanRDorDTR/content
.aspx?id=8142).

Association of American Veterinary Medical
Colleges. "Careers in Veterinary Medicine."
Retrieved October 18, 2014 (http://aavmc.org/
Students-Applicants-and-Advisors/Careers
-in-Veterinary-Medicine.aspx).

BlackPast.org. "Ross-Lee, Barbara." Retrieved
October 8, 2014 (http://www.blackpast.org/
aah/barbara-ross-lee-1942).

Brown University. "Women in Science and
Engineering Mentoring Program." Retrieved
October 16, 2014 (http://www.brown.edu/
academics/college/support/women-in-science
-and-engineering/mentoring-program).

Education Portal. "How to Become a Doctor,"
"How to Become a Climatologist," and
"Astronomer Job Information and Requirements for Students Considering a Career
in Astronomy." Retrieved October 18, 2014
(http://www.educationportal.com).

Gray, Emma. "These Stunning Photos Prove
Farmers Look Nothing Like Old MacDonald."
Huffington Post, November 20, 2013. Retrieved
October 18, 2014 (http://www.huffingtonpost
.com/2013/11/20/farmher-photos-female
-farmers-marji-guyler-alaniz_n_4304866.html).

Hannon, Kerry. "Want an Unbeatable Résumé? Read These Tips from a Top Recruiter." *Forbes*, August 24, 2011. Retrieved October 18, 2014 (http://www.forbes.com/sites/kerryhannon/2011/08/24/want-an-unbeatable-resume-read-these-tips-from-a-top-recruiter).

Institute for Food Technology. "Certified Food Scientist Eligibility." Retrieved October 17, 2014 (http://www.ift.org/Certification/ForCandidates/Eligibility.aspx).

Jane Goodall Institute. "All About Jane." Retrieved September 17, 2014 (http://www janegoodall.org/jane).

Lear, Linda. *Rachel Carson: Witness for Nature.* New York, NY: Holt, 1997.

Lewin, Tamar. "Online Mentors to Guide Women into the Sciences." *New York Times*, September 16, 2012. Retrieved October 16, 2014 (http://www.nytimes.com/2012/09/17/education/online-mentoring-program-to-encourage-women-in-sciences.html?_r=0).

Life and Legacy of Rachel Carson. "Rachel Carson's Biography." Retrieved September 17, 2014 (http://www.rachelcarson.org/Biography aspx#.VC1zYhbp_5y).

National Aeronautics and Space Administration. "Astronaut Candidate Program." Retrieved October 18, 2014 (http://astronauts.nasa.gov/content/broch00.htm).

National Library of Medicine. "Dr. Barbara Ross-Lee." Retrieved October 8, 2014 (http://www

.nlm.nih.gov/changingthefaceofmedicine/
physicians/biography_279.html).

NutritionEd.org. "Registered Dietician vs.
Dietetic Technician, Registered." Retrieved
October 17, 2014 (http://www.nutritioned.org/
rd-vs-dtr.html).

Pollack, Eileen. "Why Are There Still So Few
Women in Science?" *New York Times*, October
3, 2013. Retrieved September 10, 2014 (http://
www.nytimes.com/2013/10/06/magazine/
why-are-there-still-so-few-women-in-science
.html?pagewanted=all&_r=0).

Purdue Science. "Women in Science Programs."
Retrieved October 23, 2014 (http://www
.science.purdue.edu/wisp).

Sally Ride Science. "About Dr. Sally Ride."
Retrieved October 18, 2014 (https://
sallyridescience.com/about-us/dr-sally-ride).

Sands, David. "Female Farmer Project Shares
Stories of Women in Agriculture." Seedstock,
July 9, 2014. Retrieved October 18, 2014
(http://seedstock.com/2014/07/09/female
-farmer-project-shares-photos-stories-of
-inspiring-women).

Smith College. "Summer Science and Engineering Program." Retrieved September 15, 2014
(http://www.smith.edu/summer/programs_
ssep.php).

Vedantam, Shankar. "How Stereotypes Can
Drive Women to Quit Science." NPR, July 12,
2012. Retrieved October 23, 2014. (http://

www.npr.org/2012/07/12/156664337/stereotype
-threat-why-women-quit-science-jobs).
Washington State University School of Food
Science. "What Kind of Careers Do Food
Scientists Have?" Retrieved October 17, 2014
(http://sfs.wsu.edu/prospective-students/faq/
food-science-careers).
Willemsen, Tineke. "How Mentoring Can Help
Women Scientists." SciDev.Net. Retrieved
September 10, 2014 (http://www.scidev.net/
global/capacity-building/opinion/how
-mentoring-can-help-women-scientists-1.html).

Index

ABOUT THE AUTHOR

Rebecca T. Klein holds a B.A. in English from Marygrove College in Detroit, Michigan, and an M.A. in English/Education from Brooklyn College. She has written several books for young adults and has worked with young people for many years as a camp counselor, camp director, and teacher. All of her work is driven by her commitment to social justice and antiracism.

PHOTO CREDITS

Cover © iStockphoto.com/Susan Chiang; cover and interior pages background image © iStockphoto.com/Jamie Farrant; cover and interior pages text banners © iStockphoto.com/slav; p. 5 Paul Marotta/Getty Images; pp. 8, 9, 39 © AP Images; p. 12 Peter Muller/Cultura/Getty Images; p. 15 Sean Justice/Stone/Getty Images; p. 17 Taro Yamasaki/The Life Images Collection/Getty Images; pp. 20, 62 Monkey Business Images/Shutterstock.com; p. 24 Norberto Duarte/AFP/Getty Images; p. 27 David Gomez/E+/Getty Images; p. 30 Stock4B/Getty Images; p. 32 Penelope Breese/Liaison/Hulton Archive/Getty Images; p. 34 Les Stocker/Oxford Scientific/Getty Images; p. 37 Robbie Shone/Aurora/Getty Images; p. 41 Alfred Eisenstaedt/The Life Picture Collection/Getty Images; p. 45 NASA; p. 49 Jesse A Wanskasmith/First Light/Getty Images; p. 52 Creativa Images/Shutterstock.com; p. 54 Steve Debenport/E+/Getty Images; p. 56 Compassionate Eye Foundation/Dan Kenyon/Digital Vision/Getty Images; p. 59 The Asahi Shimbun/Getty Images; p. 63 Adam Crowley/Blend Images/Getty Images.

Designer: Nicole Russo; Editor: Meredith Day